Sullys Stick Together

DK
Editor Frankie Hallam
Project Art Editor Chris Gould
Production Editor Marc Staples
Senior Production Controller Mary Slater
Managing Editor Rachel Lawrence
Managing Art Editor Vicky Short
Managing Director Mark Searle

Designed for DK by Callum Midson
Reading Consultant Barbara Marinak

DK would like to thank Joshua Izzo at Lightstorm and Nicole Spiegel at Disney.

First American Edition, 2024
Published in the United States by DK Publishing
1745 Broadway, 20th Floor, New York, NY 10019

A catalog record for this book
is available from the Library of Congress.
ISBN 978-0-5938-4616-2 (Paperback)
ISBN 978-0-5938-4617-9 (Hardcover)

DK books are available at special discounts when purchased
in bulk for sales promotions, premiums, fund-raising, or educational use.
For details, contact: DK Publishing Special Markets,
1745 Broadway, 20th Floor, New York, NY 10019
SpecialSales@dk.com

Printed and bound in China

www.dk.com

Sullys Stick Together

Julia March

DK

Contents

Welcome to Pandora

Pandora is a moon, far away from planet Earth. Pandora is home to lots of amazing plants and animals. A species called the Na'vi lives on Pandora. They have long tails, pointed ears, and blue skin. The Sully family lives on Pandora. They are part of a forest Na'vi clan called the **Omatikaya**.

Pandora

The RDA

A group of humans called the Resources Development Administration (RDA) comes to Pandora. The RDA creates special bodies called Avatars.

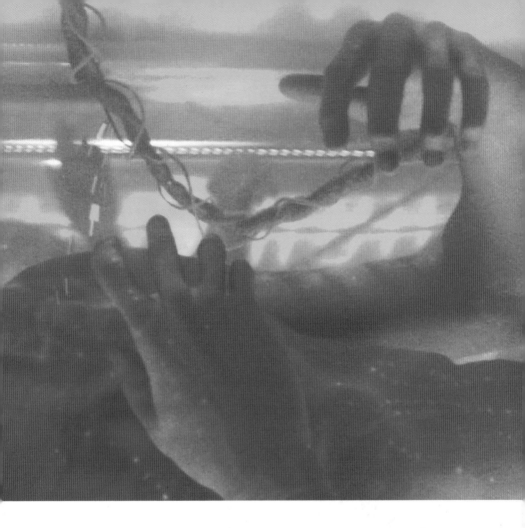

Avatars are part human and part Na'vi. Humans can move their minds into the Avatars to explore Pandora. The RDA want to take the land from the Na'vi. The Na'vi must fight to protect Pandora.

Jake Sully

Jake Sully comes to Pandora with the RDA. He uses an Avatar body to explore Pandora. Jake leaves the RDA and joins the Na'vi. He falls in love with Neytiri and they have four children.

The RDA wants to capture Jake's family. He hopes the **Metkayina** clan on the reef will help them.

Ikran rider

Some Na'vi ride flying creatures called ikran.

Neytiri

Neytiri helps Jake learn how to live in the rainforest. She is a strong warrior. Neytiri uses a bow passed on to her by her father, Eytukan. She is Jake's partner.

Neytiri accepts that leaving the Omatikaya is the best way to keep her family safe. She always puts family first.

Neytiri and her sons

Neytiri with her bow

Mo'at and Eytukan

Mo'at is Neytiri's mother. She is the Omatikaya's **tsahìk**. The tsahìk helps the clan connect with nature.

Neytiri's father, Eytukan, was a leader of the Omatikaya. He died when the RDA attacked his clan.

Eytukan's bow

Eytukan used a bow in battle. He passed it on to his daughter, Neytiri.

15

Neteyam and Lo'ak

Neteyam and Lo'ak are the two Sully boys. Neteyam is the older son. He is bold and brave. Lo'ak is the younger son. He thinks Neteyam is their dad's favorite son, but this is not true. Jake loves them equally.

Flying skills

Neteyam is good at everything he does, especially flying on his ikran.

Neteyam

Lo'ak

Tuktirey and Kiri

Tuktirey (Tuk) is the youngest Sully. Everything is a big adventure for Tuk. She easily adapts to her new life on the reef.

Her sister, Kiri, is very curious. She loves exploring the world around her.

Connected to nature

Kiri is always learning about plants and animals.

Spider

Spider is a human boy who is friends with the Sully children. He wants to be a Na'vi like them. Spider braids his hair to look like theirs.

Spider is great at climbing trees. He must wear a mask to breathe on Pandora. The air there is different than the air on earth.

Body paint

Ronal and Tonowari

Ronal and Tonowari lead the Metkayina clan. They have two children, Tsireya and Aonung. They wonder whether it is safe to let the Sullys stay with them.

Ronal

What if their guests bring trouble?

In the end they agree to help.

Skimwing

Tonowari rides on an animal called a skimwing.

Tonowari

Tsireya and Aonung

Aonung is the son of Tonowari and Ronal. He does not like the Sullys at first.

His sister, Tsireya, is kinder. She teaches the Sully kids how to live on the reef. They learn how to ride an animal called an **ilu**.

Seashell armband

Aonung

New friend

Tsireya teaches Lo'ak how to hold his breath underwater.

Tsireya

Payakan

Flipper

Fin

Payakan is an underwater creature called a **tulkun**. The Metkayina say he is dangerous, but Lo'ak thinks he is kind. Lo'ak and Payakan become friends.

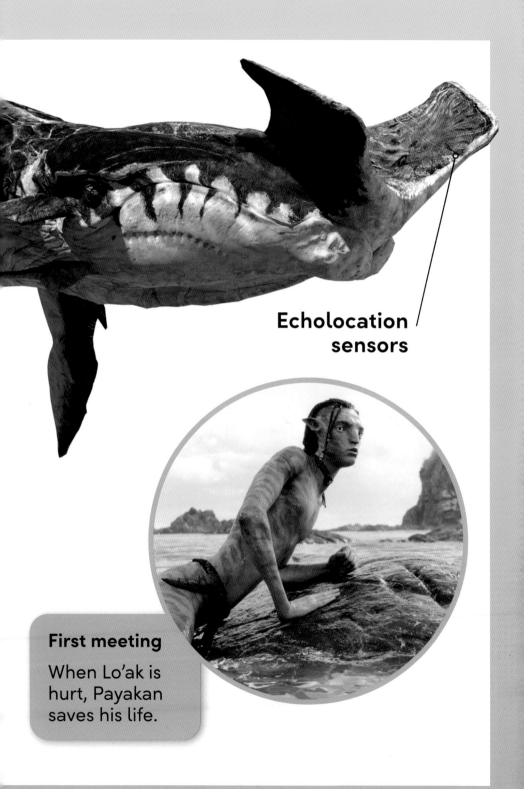

Echolocation sensors

First meeting

When Lo'ak is hurt, Payakan saves his life.

Family is our fortress

When things seem tough, the Sullys know they can always rely on one another. As Jake Sully often says, "Family is our fortress." This means that they always protect each other.

Glossary

Avatar
A human whose mind has been moved into a Na'vi body so they can breathe and move around easily on Pandora.

Clan
A large family group whose members live together and follow the same customs.

Echolocation
A way of working out how far away something is using sounds and vibrations.

Ikran
A flying creature. The Omatikaya ride ikran to travel long distances or to hunt.

Ilu
A sea reptile with flippers and a long, bendy neck. The Metkayina ride on ilu. They are friendly and easy to tame.

Metkayina
A Na'vi clan that lives on the reef on Pandora.

Na'vi
A species native to Pandora. Na'vi have tails and blue skin. They are much taller than humans. Na'vi live in separate clans on different parts of Pandora.

Omatikaya
A Na'vi clan that lives in the rainforests of Pandora. The Omatikaya use bows and arrows to hunt and fight.

RDA
RDA is short for Resources Development Administration. Its members are humans who have traveled from Earth to Pandora. They want to fight the Na'vi and take over their land.

Reef
A line of rocks or sand at the edge of the sea.

Skimwing
A large sea creature a little like a flying fish. The Metkayina ride skimwings to fly above the water or dive under it.

Tsahìk
A Na'vi who has a special link with nature and performs clan rituals. Each clan has just one tsahìk.

Tulkun
An intelligent whalelike creature that lives in the seas of Pandora.

Index

NA'VI WORD PRONUNCIATION GUIDE

Ikran is pronounced EEK-RAHN
Ilu is pronounced EE-LOO
Metkayina is pronounced MET-KAH-YEE-NAH
Na'vi is pronounced NA-VEE
Omatikaya is pronounced O-MAH-TEE-KAH-YAH
Tsahìk is pronounced TSAH-HEEK
Tulkun is pronounced TOOL-KOON

Quiz

Ready to find out how much you learned?
Read the questions below and write
down each answer. Then check your work
against the answer key at the bottom of
the page.

1. What clan does the Sully family
    belong to?

2. Who was Eytukan?

3. How is Spider able to breathe on
    Pandora?

4. Where on Pandora does the
    Metkayina clan live?

5. What kind of creature is Payakan?

Answers: 1. Omatikaya 2. Neytiri's father 3. He wears a mask 4. On the reef 5. A tulkun